Blockchain:

Simple Solution to US Debt Crisis
'Leverage Debt Reduction'

(Block-Chain for Financial Sector)

As Leverage Financing has done for investments,

Leverage Debt Reduction will do for Debt.

Raghu Giuffre

Rough Draft:
Ready for Editorial Review,
Proofreader & Citations

Occupy The Highway demonstrator Bo Han (left) is greeted by fellow marcher Raghu Giuffre as they arrive in McPherson Square in Washington on Tuesday.

Manuel Balce Ceneta Associated Press

Protesters walk to Washington

Group from Manhattan arrives in capital city after two-week journey

By Ben Nuckols
Associated Press

WASHINGTON | Drenched, blistered and weary, a few dozen Occupy Wall Street protesters arrived Tuesday in the nation's capital after a two-week, 240-mile march from Zuccotti Park in lower Manhattan.

The marchers, many wearing hooded ponchos in a steady rain, walked into the Occupy D.C. encampment, where fellow protesters lined up outside their tents and greeted them with cheers, applause and hugs.

Organizers said the march, which they called Occupy the Highway, accomplished their goal of taking their concerns about income equality and corporate influence in politics on the road, including to rural communities that previously had little exposure to the movement.

"People who had never heard about the occupation, heard about it," said Owen Johnson, 23, an artist from North Pownal, Vt., who walked the entire distance barefoot, suffering only a few cuts on his feet.

The march covered about 20 miles a day. Participants spent a few nights at protest encampments in other cities.

They also slept on college campuses and in the homes of supporters, churches, a music studio and a community center.

About two dozen people left Zuccotti Park for the march, and while not all of those made it to Washington, by the final day the crowd had swelled to more than 40, organizer Kelley Brannon said. The crowd size fluctuated throughout, as some joined the march for brief periods.

Not all made the trip unscathed. One had to quit because of shin splints, others because of illness. A marcher was hit by a car Monday night but still made it to Washington.

The march was timed to coincide with the conclusion of work by the congressional deficit-cutting supercommittee. Participants wanted to push for an end to Bush-era tax cuts that benefit the wealthy.

The supercommittee announced Monday it had failed to reach an agreement, and marchers said they weren't surprised.

"It was set up to fail. They were never going to get anything done," Aldous said.

Introduction

Raghu-nomics estimates that 20% to 80% of all US debt does not actually exist (depending upon the industry). We refer to this as *Phantom Debt*.

We give the example of parents co-signing a student loan of $50k for their college bound boy. This same $50k would be reflected in both parent's credit scores. This would now give the impression of $150k worth of total debt to an outsider auditor – *'Expert.'* We refer to the parent's loan as *Mirror Debts*. A payment on that student loan would also be reflected to the parent's credit referred to as a *Double Paydown* and *Leverage Debt Reduction*.

Our case is simple. Wall Street has created a series of products that are little more than duplicate *Mirror Debts*. Surprisingly, there is no tracking system to cross index all these *Mirror Debts* or follow payments made to one and credit to all the others. We do have this for a student loan, but not for Wall Street.

In the case of 2008, we counted 11 Mirror Debts for our home mortgage. They were rebranded under such headings as Securitized Debt, Securitized Mortgages, Credit Default Swaps and finally, US Bonds. Each of them also had their own set of *Double Paydowns*. Those were also never credited from one product platform to the others. Doing so would have erased up to 150% of all so-called debts from a cross section of Wall Street industries. For example, up to $5 trillion of today's federal deficits are in fact a *Phantom Debt* and likely paid-off long ago.

A blockchain system is a rather simple remedy that would have sidestepped much of the 2008 market meltdown. Implementing Leverage Debt Reduction today would up-grade our entire financial system. It would function like an insurance program against any number of prospective threats to our financial system. Welcome to Leverage Debt Reduction.

Volume 13 of Raghu-nomics is a re-write of Volume 2: RADHA Mortgage -Simple Solution to Real Estate Crisis (2008); and Volume 4 Leverage Debt Reduction (2010). These two volumes presented the problems and solutions to the real estate crisis of 2008. It took the advent of Blockchain before we had an easily definable technology to point to implement our proposed insurance program that could handle the demands of today's financial markets. We now beget: Blockchain, Simple Solution to US Debt Crisis.

(Front Cover: I joined the Occupy Wall Street movement for about 2 month in the hope of connecting with activist or media interested in solutions to the real estate crisis. It culminated with their march from NY to DC: Front page Newspaper article. I found now interest in media or Occupy clan so I returned to Hawaii and ran for Congress. This was one of a number of campaigns tried to draw attention to Leverage Debt Reduction - simple solution to these financial crisis.)

1st Draft completed July 4th, 2019, In Manoa, Honolulu, at the residence of Divona Cox.

Table of Contents

Part 1: Wall Street

Chapter 1   Mirror Debt & Double Pay-downs: $5 Trillion in Federal Deficits - Erased 6

Chapter 2 ,,,,Secondary Insurance for Capital Markets 12

Chapter 3 ,,,,Secondary Market for Gov't 14

Chapter 4   5 Advantages for Provider...16

Chapter 5   Phantom Debt 18

Chapter 6   Leverage Financing in Reverse; Antidote to Derivatives..................20

Chapter 7   The 'Write-down;' Lehman: $780 Trillion in *Double Pay-downs* 22

Chapter 8   Bank of Grandma...24

Chapter 9   Credit Defaults Swaps: Easy 1st Step 25

Chapter 10   11 Mirror Debts of Real Estate Market..26

Chapter 11   Finding 'The 7 Partners'...28

Chapter 12   4 Different Groups, Same Mortgage..30

Chapter 13   US Bonds; $5 Trillion of Fed Deficits in Mirror Debts 33

Chapter 14   Unraveling the Debt Crisis...34

Chapter 15 $5 Trillion in US Deficits – Wiped Clean; Tracking Double-Paydowns 36

Chapter 16   Tap Trillions in Savings: Refinance Entire Market;

Part 2 Main Street

Chapter 17   Avatar Loans: Leverage Financing in Blue Collar Industries...........40

Chapter 18   Untangle Hidden Values Behind Debt 43

Chapter 19   VALDOS vs LIDOS: Value-Debts vs Liability Debts 46

Chapter 20   More Tools for More Market Bubbles: To be Re-written and Misc Notes 54

Part 1: Wall Street

Chapter 1

Mirror Debt & Double Pay-downs

$5 Trillion in Federal Deficits - Erased

'Leverage Debt Reduction:' Paying Multiple debts w/ 1 payment

'Leverage Debt Reduction' means paying off multiple debts when you make a payment on just one debt. The acronym is LeDeR – *'LEDER.'*

'Mirror Debt'

Let's use the example of a student loan. Say your mom and dad co-signed a student loan for you. The loan is for $50,000 ($50k).

You, your mom and your dad will have this same $50k worth of debt showing-up on each of your individual credit reports. The reports will show that each of you now carry $50k worth of debt. We refer to this as *'Mirror Debts.'* It means when the SAME debt shows up on multiple accounts under different names.

'Expert Reading'

Let's introduce our investment *'Expert.'* He's *'Reading'* over these 3 credit reports. Let's also say he didn't recognize that these 3 accounts were all related to the same family or the SAME student loan. He overlooked this common link. This leaves the *'Expert'* to think these are 3 separate loans for $50k. He, therefore, counts that $50k debt three times. Once for you and again for your mom and then your dad too. By the *Experts Reading* (calculation), there is $150,000 worth of debt.

Here, we know he is wrong. There is only $50k. He failed to see the LINK between you and your parents. So, he counted that same $50k three times. He missed that they were the SAME loan *'Re-listed'* under 3 different names.

$50k – Your Student Loan

$50k – Co-signer 1: Mom; Mirror Debt 1

$50k – Co-signer 2: Dad; Mirror Debt 2

$150k – Expert thinks each debt is a separate and unrelated loan rather than recognizing that two of these are co-signers to the first original debt.

Today's *Experts* are making this same mistake again. They tell us about the billions (trillions) America has piled-up in debt. Much of that is in *Mirror Debts*. It's the same debt being counted multiple times – under different headings.

I discovered this while studying the Credit Default Swap market back in 2007 - 09. Back then, the same debt had **11 DIFFERENT *MIRROR DEBTS*** – covered in Chapters 6 - 9.

'Double Pay-down'

Here's were *LEDER (Leverage Debt Reduction)* comes into play. Let's say you pay-off $20,000 worth of your Student Loan. That will also pay down the debts listed under your parents accounts as well. Each of you will show this same $20k debt reduction on your respective credit reports.

The *Expert* first thought there was $150,000 in combined debt. He again looks over those same credit reports after your payment. He now sees the combined debt of just $90k.

You paid-off $60k worth of debts by making a $20k payment on your own Student Loan. Those reports applied this same $20k to all the accounts: yours, your mom's and your dads. By the *Experts Reading* there is $60k worth of repayments made against the original $150k.

This is an example of how *LEDER* works. You only paid on one account. That SAME payment showed up on all 3 accounts. We refer to this as a '**Double Pay-down**.' A *Double Pay-down* is the secret behind *LEDER*.

The same is true when your mom makes a payment on the loan listed under her name. True again for your dad. Payments made by your parents go towards the loan listed under your credit report too.

$20k – Amount You paid on your Original Student Loan;
$20k – Payment shows on the loan listed under Mom's accounts;
$20k - Payment shows on the loan listed under Dad's accounts;
$60k – Total Paid according to *Expert Reading* of the 3 Accounts;
$90k – Remaining Debt of the 3 different accounts as *Read* by the *Expert*.
.   This is down from a total debt of $150k.

Problem & Solution – Track Payments to All *Mirror Debts*

We find *Mirror Debts* throughout most financial markets. That is multiplied – exponentially - in derivatives markets. All these markets are counting the same (Mirror) debt, multiple times. They do so under different headings and players. These different players are also making various payments on their respective debt obligations. Each of these payments should be going to paydown the debts on a host of other *Mirror Debts*. But...

The Problem:

You may have guessed the problem - as we see it. All those different payments (made on all the different *Mirror Debts*) are not being tracked (in today's financial markets). A great example is *Credit Default Swaps*. There are many others.

Missing the link between *Mirror Debts* is the first problem.

Failing to tack all the different payments to each *Mirror Debt* is the second problem.

Failing to credit those payments from one account to the others is the third problem.

Our video may have said it best: The 2008 real estate crisis was "one big accounting mistake."

'Deleveraging Debt'

Applying this system of *Leverage Debt Reduction* is referred to as *'Deleveraging Debt*.' It's the process of *Leverage Debt Reduction*. It pays down loans at an accelerated (multiplied) rate of debt reduction.

Blockchain: Chronicle of Debt Ledgers – C-Dels

LEDER (Leverage Debt Reduction) introduces the need for a program that can track all these corresponding *Mirror Debts*. The program would record the payments made on any given *Mirror Debt*. It than applies that SAME credit to all the other counter-part *Mirror Debts*.

Put simply, today's financial markets need a blockchain tracking system. We need a service to chronicle and track all the corresponding '*Debt Ledgers*.' We call it '*Chronicle of Debt Ledgers – C-Dels*.'

C-Dels tracking system would work much like your student loan cosigned by mom and dad. Their loans are reduced along with your payments - automatically. And visa-versa.

A large part of today's financial markets are made of *Mirror Debts*. Therefore, most financial markets offer this same kind of *Double Pay-down*. Later chapters demonstrate how *LEDER* could have reduced market losses to just 1% the markets value compared to the 85% losses we saw of 2008. (Chapter 14)

GOOD NEWS: AMERICA MAY HAVE 20% TO 70% LESS DEBT then we presently have been led to believe. (Amounts varies by industry.)

A prime example is today's federal deficits. Up to $5 trillion of today's deficits are from the 2008 gov't 'bail-outs' of US banks. That banking bail-out was mostly made of *Mirror Debts*. In other words,

UPTO $5 TRILLION OF TODAY'S FEDERAL DEFICITS MAY HAVE ALREADY BEEN PAID OFF – LONG AGO.

We will be covering that shortly. Trillions of today's fed deficits are made of these banking bailouts. Most of those securities had already taken a number of *Double Paydowns* before they were give over to the gov't. We simply need to track their counter-parts and credit the '*Double Paydown*.' This is just one example of how *C-Dels* would help reduce US debt – starting with the $5 trillion of fed deficits.

We cover how and why this happened and some simple steps to tap it for extra-ordinary debt reduction. The simple answer is Blockchain. It may have found the magic wand of debt reduction.

Welcome to *Leverage Debt Reduction*.

The Answer: You

Have you ever found people asking with suspicion or just befuddled:

Where does all this debt come from?

How do we have so much debt?

Who has all this debt?

Now you know the answer.

It's you and all your *Mirror Debts*.

The following YouTube Video was made in 2012 based upon the books written in 2008 called – the RADHA Mortgage: Simple Solution to Real Estate Crisis. We have up-graded the concept and program since then.

https://www.youtube.com/watch?v=UOwIkiJRPa8&t=2s

Leverage Debt Reduction: LEDER	*'Double Pay-down'*
'Mirror Debt'	*'Deleveraging Debt'*
'Expert Reading'	*Chronicle of Debt Ledgers – C-Dels*
'Re-listed'	

Chapter 2

Secondary Insurance for Capital Markets

'Secondary Market Provider'

We are pointing out the need for a new industry player. They would track all **Mirror Debts** and corresponding **Double Pay-downs**. They would be keepers of the '**Chronicle of Debt Ledgers or C-Dels**.' (Last Chapter)

The purpose of *C-Dels* is to provide a new insurance service. This service would be a secondary insurer like we see of Warren Buffet. He insures the insurance companies.

Warren Buffet is referred to as the **'Secondary-Market'** of the insurance industry. The provider of *C-Dels'* would be the Warren Buffet of the financial sector.

We refer to this function as a **'Secondary Market Provider.'** Here's their role in today's insurance industry:

Let's take the example of a local insurance company from California. Let's say they were hit with the cost of a local earthquake. Warren Buffet steps-in and provides that insurance company with additional capital. This keeps that local insurance company financially solvent.

This California company is referred to as a **'Retail Insurance'** company. They are part of the **'retail market.'** Warren Buffet helps them cover the cost of insurance claims from that earthquake. His company is the *Secondary-Market* of the insurance industry.

Warren Buffet evens-out the industry as a whole. On the one side, he collects and pools income from other 'retail' insurance companies from across the nation. He then uses that revenue to help the California insurance company. We need this same kind of provider for capital markets.

We demonstrate some ways this cold work. (Chapters 10 – 18) The 'how-to' becomes more obvious once we recognize this common link of *Mirror Debts* between companies and industries. It all starts with understanding *Mirror Debts*.

Chapter 3

Secondary Market for Gov't

Save Gov't, Reduce Bail-outs

The *Secondary-Market Provider* is the back-up to 'retail insurance' companies. (Last Chapter) It covers *Retailers* when they are over-exposed to local disasters. This arrangement also buffers the gov't as well.

The *Secondary Market* offers gov't critical savings on two fronts:

a) Reduces the number of times gov't must step-in to bailout the industry;
b) Reduces the amounts required of the gov't when they must step-in with a bailout.

The gov't is there when the *Secondary Provider* can't afford to cover all the costs themselves. The cost of gov't bailouts is far greater without these *Secondary Providers*. This is even more true of financial markets. They need these Providers as much as the gov't.

By our estimates, a *Secondary-Market Provider* would have covered much of the market melt-down of 2008 – by 90% (Chapter 12). Even if there had been some shortfall, the money required would be a fraction those we saw of the gov't's 2008 bailouts. (Chapter 12)

Here's another way of saying this:

OUR FINANCIAL SYSTEM HAD BUILT A SURPRISINGLY STRONG, SERIES OF SAFETY-GUARDS TO HANDLE ANY NUMBER OF MARKET CORRECTIONS. Here's the great news. We already have this impressive infrastructure in place. A *Secondary-Market Provider* can plug into that pre-existing system. It requires little more than formalizing this great infrastructure that is all set up and ready to go.

For example, **Credit Default Swaps** were fashioned to serve this very purpose – among other financial products. (Chapter 6.) *Credit Default Swaps* already have the capital pools in place to tap – among other resources. The primary step missing is a blockchain-like tracking system to coordinate this kind of operation. This last step should prove relatively simple, fast and easy when talking of launching a trillion-dollar industry.

A number of financial markets would benefit from a *Secondary-Market Provider*. This would buffer (save) the 'Retail-Market' of investments (Wall Street) and allow the industry to become much more self-sustaining. Same is true for the gov't. *LEDER* would do wonders for both the market as well as the gov't.

Chapter 4

5 Advantages for Provider

4 Advantages: Size, Risk, Power

A *Secondary-Market Provider* would do for financial markets as Warren Buffet's does for retail insurance companies. (Chapter 2) However, there are 5 advantages in serving financial market over those covered by Warren Buffet:

1) The first advantage is size. It starts with trillions rather than billions. ($65 Trillion for the Credit Defaults Swaps market alone – it's about a third that today. 80% of that was *Mirror Debts.*)

2) A much larger pool of financial safety valves – buffers – compared to Warren Buffet's *Secondary Market* sector. (The 2008 market had 11 *Mirror Debts* to pool from. Warren Buffet could only dream of having such an infrastructure to call upon.)

3) Likely become the primary player to their respective industry.

4) Likely become a gate-keeper of their market.

5) Used more often – more relevant.

The *Secondary-Market Providers* would have..

a) far greater revenues,
b) (likely) less risk, and probably,
c) more market power, and
d) larger role,

..than we see of Warren Buffet. Companies such as Goldman Sachs are well suited for the role. We are searching for a company interested in looking into such a project. Would love to connect with Goldman Sachs.

Chapter 5

Phantom Debt

Phantom Debt

Today's system makes it easy to track payments on a co-signed student loan. There is no such system to track all the *Mirror Debts* for industries like *Credit Default Swaps*. Missing this critical step (of a tracking system creates a massive façade of '**Phantom-Debt**.'

Much of this so-called debt does not exist. It's a massive façade overlaid upon all areas of life in America. In the case of 2008, it gave the appearance of tens of trillions of liability – most of that was in *Phantom Debt*. The debt didn't actually exist.

It's just like that $50k student loan mentioned in Chapter 1. The *'Expert'* thought there was $150k worth of debts. He was wrong. There was the original $50k student loan - only. That same loan was simply reflected in each of your family's 3 accounts (once your parents co-signed the loan for you). Your parents served as a back-up - guarantor - for that loan. That last $100k was all *Phantom Debt*.

There is one big difference between your parents and Wall Street. Wall Street actually paid on each of their respective (Mirror) debts. It would be like your parents also paying on your student loan the same time you are. This *Double Paydown* reduces debt very quickly. Once again, the problem: None of those payments were tracked and registered to their counter-part *Mirror Debts*.

The net result is obvious. *Phantom Debt* creates massive market distortions. It gives the impression we have far more debt than what really exist. **LEDER** *(Leverage Debt Reduction)* cuts through all the fluster, falsehood and confusion.

A new clarity will uncover hidden values otherwise buried under the *Experts* dreadfully inaccurate (mis)*Reading*. The *11 Mirror Debts* of Chapter... captures the point. It gives some hint to all the streams of revenue and veins of asset value running throughout the system - just waiting to be discovered via a *C-Del* system.

Chapter 6

Leverage Financing in Reverse

Antidote to Derivatives

Here's another way to explain Leverage Debt Reduction. Most people heard of Leverage Financing. Let's use the example of $100. Let's say Leverage Financing of $100 would buy $500 worth of investments. (It's often more, but a detail for another time.) You may only have $100, but you can buy $500 worth of investments using Leverage Financing.

Antidote to Derivatives

LEDER (Leverage Debt Reduction) reverses this process. The reverse of this means that paying one debt can pay-off multiple other debts too. In other words, the leverage process works both ways. You can Leverage your money to buy multiple investments on the same dollar. You can also leverage your money to repay multiple debts as well. The leverage process is a two-way street (system). The other side of Leverage Financing is *Leverage Debt Reduction – 'De-Leveraging Debt.'*

The big surprise here is that this process will often have a much larger impact at 'De-leveraging Debt' then it does at leveraging investment. (Will explain why in later chapters.) In other words, financial leveraging allows you to pay-off more debt than it can buy in investments. Put another way, *Leverage Debt Reduction* is likely to be a SIGNIFICNATLY larger market over today's market for Leverage Financing.

For example, you may be able to buy $500 worth of investment by leveraging $100 worth of capital. (Working figures.) However, you can pay-off a lot more debt with that same $100 in payments. More specifically, $100 worth of *Leverage Debt Reduction* would have paid off $1,100 worth of debt back in 2008. (True figure.) Chapter 5 and 9

We may have found the market cure at long last:

LEVERAGE DEBT REDUCTION MAY PROVE THE ANTIDOTE TO TODAY'S DERIVITIVES MARKET.

Whatever the case maybe, we introduce you to the other side of leveraged financing with this *Leverage Debt Reduction*. This discovery will do for debt as Leverage Financing has done for investing and Wall Street.

Chapter 7

The 'Write-down'

Lehman: $780 Trillion in *Double Pay-downs*

Lehman Brothers: $780 Trillion in *Double Write-downs*

Lehman Brothers was a big Wall Street trading firm. The company went from a worth of $800 billion down to just $20 billion in about 3 weeks. Their collapse set off the market crash of 2008.

Their $780 billion in 'lost' value actually represented this massive *Double Write-down*. This debt reduction simply needed to be applied to all the other companies carrying counter-part *Mirror Debts*. We will explain this shortly. For now, the point is that this was a giant debt reduction and should have represented a positive step rather than the tipping point into a terrible market implosion.

Here's our rough estimate:

That $780 billion loss to Lehman would have a *Double Write-down* value of 5 to 10 times that amount - once reflected across all *Mirror Debts*. That is $3.5 trillion to $8 trillion worth of *Double Write-downs*. More on that shortly. For now, understand the concept of a 'Write-down.'

Pay Difference between Debt and Market Value

A *'Write-down'* means you pay out of pocket. The money is used to pay the difference between the sales price of an asset and the amount still owed on it.

How Write-downs (should) work

Let's use the example of a car.

You bought a car, but still owe $10,000 on it.

However, no one would buy it for more than $6,000.

If you wanted to sell the car; you pay $4,000 to the bank holding the pink-slip.

This $4,000 comes from your own pocket.

That's a **WRITE-DOWN**.

You can than sell the car for the remaining $6,000.

Banks are required to do the same with their assets before they sell them. Banks were facing a cash crunch in 2008. They had to sell assets to build cash reserves. The bank paid the difference between what was owed on their asset, over what it could be sold for – the market value.

(The Market Value is in how much a third party is willing to pay for it.)

Banks took these big *write-downs* - worth (hundreds) billions. They had counter-part *Mirror Debts*. Therefore, each new write-down offered 5x to 10x that amount in *Double Paydowns*. This gives us some idea how much *LEDER* could have helped offset the 2008 meltdown. (Details..Chapter...)

Chapter 8

Bank of Grandma

Bank of Grandma

We hear about banks and investment firms taking all these 'big write-downs.' For Lehman Brothers, it was $780 billion. But here's the odd thing. Lehman didn't have any money of their own. In function, Lehman was really just a financial asset management company. The money - asset - was held by a third party.

So how could they make any kind of write-down?

The money belonged to a third party. Who was this third party?

It was your 401K - Your life savings.

My Mom's 401k fell from $100k to $50k in about a year. She lost about half all her life savings.

Yeap, my Mom was often the only, one true 'investor' standing behind Lehman.

Who would have thought?

Much of that money came from my Mom and all the other grandmas from around the world. Grandma was the bank. Wall Street used grandma's money for all their gambling bets. In function and purpose, Grandma was the real the bank. We should just call it the Bank of Grandma.

That's why my Mom took the losses on the home mortgage investment. So did all the other millions of Americans with a 401K. They lost much of their life savings too.

Anyway....Some of that value can still be recouped. More on that shortly. For now, let's begin by identifying all the different *Mirror Debts* at play in our financial system. Credit Default Swaps is a good place to start. Next.

Chapter 9

Credit Defaults Swaps: Easy 1st Step

Credit Default Swaps: Insurance Policy to Build-on

Credit Defaults carry one of the largest multipliers of *Mirror Debt*. It has also been crafted to serve as an insurance program. It therefore offers a great place to begin our review.

A *'Credit Default Swap'* – is referred to as a *'CDS.'* Basically, it's an insurance policy for investors. CDS's offer to insure *'Mortgage-backed Securities.'* These Securities pooled thousands of home mortgages together into one big package. This package was then sold to investors. Let's say the home buyer stops paying and defaults on their mortgage. The investor is reimbursed by his *CDS* insurance policy.

The *CDS* market can appear like some 'exotic' derivatives market (and for good reason – Chapter..). However, the actual function of *CDS* is fairly straight forward. It works like most kinds of insurance. The *CDS* policy reimburses investors against losses to their asset. In this case, the asset is a *Mortgage-backed-Security (aka. Securitized Mortgage)*.

CDS is an insurance policy offered to cover *Securitized Mortgages* and to investors who buy them. This function presents a natural platform to build-out a broader market insurance program. It's already been tailored to serve as an insurance-like *Secondary-Market Provider*. The missing step is a block-chain tracking system (we call it *C-Del: Chronicle of Debt Ledgers*).

CDS (Credit Default Swaps) simply needs to begin coordinating the (dozen) partners of *Mirror Debts*. Today's *CDS* market is one step away from being a Secondary Insurance program. *C-Del* offers that final step to their role as this new industry – a blockchain tracking system.

Chapter 10

11 Mirror Debts of Real Estate Market

5 Credit Default Swaps Per Mortgage

This brings us back to that investment '*Expert*' mentioned in Chapter 1. Let's say the *Expert* is talking about $150,000 in **Credit Default Swaps** or **CDS** (last chapter). We now know it's much like the student loan that was co-signed by your two parents (Chapter 1).

The *Expert* mis-counted your student loan. There was just $50k worth of debt, NOT the $150k he thought. $100k of that debt was all *Phantom Debt*. The same happened with the *CDS* market.

Back in 2008, the *Experts* estimated that there was 5 *CDS*. Specifically, they calculated $65 trillion in *Credit Default Swaps*. Compare this to the $12 trillion in home mortgages.

CDS were intended to cover these mortgages, but there was 5 such policies for every home mortgage. How can there be 5 times more insurance policies then there are units it is suppose to insure? OBVIOUSLY, most of this was in *Mirror Debts*. There is no such thing as $65 trillion worth of debt for any given industry in America. Welcome to *Mirror Debts* and *Phantom Debts*. And this was for only one industry. Every other industry of the financial markets had their own set of *Mirror Debts* too. Most of it *Phantom Debt* too.

This introduces several things – all of which present us with incredible prospects.

1) That gives us 5 *Mirror Debt* (obligations) for every mortgage in the country.
   - 80% of that market was / is *Phantom Debt*. This means **we can use 5 as the multiplier for calculating *Double Pay-downs.*** *CDS* starts us with a multiplier of 5. Fascinating how this translates into calculating De-leveraging Debt. (How this works and its advantages outlined in Chapters ….)

2) The *CDS* market also provided the equivalent of 5 insurance policies for every home mortgage in America.
   -Most mortgages had been entirely repaid once we credit the *Double Paydown* from *CDS* write-downs. Chapters…

3) Your home had 5 warranties or co-signers to your mortgage.
   - Each new co-signer brings one more market dynamic – advantage. For example, each was paying annually on their respective asset. This offers a multiplied value and paydown. Think of it as building equity in your mortgage much much faster. Chapters.

6 Other Partners = 10 Partners

There is a whole other set of *Mirror Debts*. This is on top the 5 we get from *CDS* policies. This other set is from 6 more 'new' Partners. Each Partner had their own set of *Mirror Debts*. We now have the 5 *CDS* policies PLUS the 6 other parties more from this new group of Partners.

Behold: 11 *Mirror Debts* in total - for every home mortgage in America (back in 2008). Think of it as 11 'co-signers' to your home mortgage. Let's introduce these 6 new Partners. Next Chapter.

Chapter 11

Finding 'The 7 Partners'

10 Mirror Debts of Real Estate

Here's the list of 10 *Mirror Debts*.

1) **CDS (#1 - #5 Mirror Debts)**
   We had the 5 *CDS* (insurance policies) for every home mortgage in America. (Last Chapter)

2) **First Mortgage (#6 Mirror Debt)**
   We had the first home mortgage itself - held by the homeowner. That gives us 6 *Mirror Debts*.

3) **Second Mortgage (#7 Mirror Debt)**
   There was the 2nd Mortgage. This was on top the 1st Mortgage. That gives us 7 *Mirror Debts*.

4) **PMI (#8 Mirror Debt)**
   There was the PMI insurance that covers any loss on the 2nd Mortgage. (Explained shortly – Chapter....) That is 8 *Mirror Debts*.

5) **Mortgage Backed Securities (#9 Mirror Debt)**
   Home mortgages were pooled together and sold to investors as ***'Securitized Mortgages.'*** These investors added one more partner (co-signer) to the real estate (process). These were insured by *CDS* – above.

6) **401K (Bank of Grandma) (#10 Mirror Debt)**

A big part of our 401K retirement savings was made of *Securitized Mortgages* – back in 2008. All those so-called 'market losses' are a Wall Street euphemism for the pillage and plunder of Grandma's lifesavings. It also means your mortgage and Grandma's 401K are the same thing. In other words, Grandma is your banker. More on that later.

7) **US Bonds (Gov't Bail-outs) (#11 Mirror Debt)**

Gov't bailed-out the banks in 2008. They did so through a variety of programs over the next (half) decade. There was the direct bailout of 2008. Additional bailout followed by the Federal Reserve and again by the US Treasury. They repackaged these programs as Quantitative Easying – among others. More details later. The point: The gov't repackaged these *Securitized Mortgages* and renamed them US Bonds.

This gives us 11 *Mirror Debts*. Each new Partner serving as one more back-up to the same asset – your home (mortgage). Next Chapter. We will also find how each new *Mirror Debt* is a multiplier to our debt reduction as well as adding one more value to the asset.

Once combined, you beget an EXPONENTIAL impact upon debt reduction and value creation.

More on that later..Chapter

Following these 7 partners will help clarify the convoluted journey of America's mortgage Wall Street process. It's more an eco-system in contrast to some random series of financial products – as often portrayed. They are not. Each product is - literally - an extension of the product (program) that comes just before it. We therefore track each player to see how they work together to form but a single process. This will help map an effective tracking system – *C-DELS*.

Such a map will show us how a blockchain would work. For example, it's likely better to have all *CDS's* coordinated as part of a single insurance program. Such a program would handle most major market 'corrections.' And so it begins with our 7 *Partners* and 4 *Different Groups:* Next Chapter

Chapter 12

4 Different Groups, Same Mortgage

6 Partners; 4 Groups

We finally arrive at our working model. The first step is to identify all the different parties or partners linked to the home mortgage.

These parties are referred to as *"Partners."*

There are 7 primary *Partners* (to these 11 *Mirror Debts - last chapter)*

These *Partners* specialize in 4 different areas of the mortgage process. Each of these areas form their own *Group of Partners*.

This may sound like a lot of info, but these are players you are already familiar with such as a home mortgage, 2nd mortgage, 401k or gov't bonds. Now for the first time, you will get to see how they all come together as part of a single system.

The *First Group* of *Partners* work with the homeowner. They cover the home mortgage side of the industry. We list the names of different companies. Each of them specialized in their area of the market back in 2008. The named companies give us a face to track through each step of this 'journey of mortgages.'

Group 1; Home Mortgage: 3 Partners (#1 thru #3)

1) Wells Fargo – 1st Mortgage (80% of the loan).
2) Chase Manhattan – 2nd Mortgage. (Covers the first 20% of losses).
3) AIG: - PMI Insurance. Insures 2nd mortgage for Chase Manhattan against 100% of any losses on the 2nd mortgage.

The **Second Group** is Wall Street. They bundle lots of mortgages into great, big packages and sell them off as investments. Often, mortgages are 'spliced and diced' into these little pieces. I call it 'asset dismemberment.' It is the centerpiece of Wall Street's 'toxic mess of mass confusion.' – once markets start going South. *C-Dels*, a blockchain, will crack this 'financial black-hole of Wall Street.' It will save the trillions now lost in their **MARKET MUTATIONS OF MASS DESTRUCTION**.

Group 2; Wall Street: 2 Partners (#4 – #5)

4) Goldman Sachs – *'Mortgage Backed Securities'* (aka. *Securitized Mortgages*).
5) Lehman Brothers – *CDS (Credit Default Swaps)* Insurance Policy for *Securitize Mortgages*.

The **Third Group of Partners** is made of our retirements. Our 401k savings accounts were stuffed with *Mortgage Backed Securities*. Wall Street banks have been using our 401k's to cover their stock market casino bets. This is an obvious 'abuse of power' and a 'conflict of interest,' but this also has the effect of converting our 401k's into the actual bank holder behind these assets. Banks no longer carry these assets. You do. All those with 401ks.

WALL STREET BANKS HAVE INADVERTENTLY MADE OUR 401K THE LEGITIMATE OWNER OF THESE MORTGAGES. Banks have given over the home mortgage to us in every way but in name. Taking claim to the actual mortgage itself, would be a natural market based reform to Wall Street's abuse and market distortion....chapter

Group 3; 401 K Grandma's Retirement: 1 Partner (#6)

6) Charles Swab.

The **Fourth Group of Partners** is the gov't. Those different real estate products were 'bought' by the gov't. It was done in a series of different bail-out programs - ex: *Quantitative Easying*, etc. The gov't bought up to $5 TRILLION in *Securitized Mortgages & CDS*. These securities were then re-branded as '**US Bonds**.' Those *Bonds* now stand as part of today's Federal Deficits.

Group 4; US Bonds (Bail-outs): 1 Partner (#7)

7) US Bonds & Quantitative Easing,

We are going to jump straight to *US Bonds* for our example on how *LEDER (Leverage Debt Reduction)* could impact debt reduction. This step of the process gives the easiest example to explain. This step is also quite dramatic in how much debt is canceled - $5 trillion. The impact is multiplied because US Bonds are the last step in this system. Therefore, they include all the other *'Double Paydowns'* by each of the earlier *Partners* of the process. Explained next.

Chapter 13

US Bonds:

$5 Trillion of Fed Deficits in Mirror Debts

Fed Deficits of Mirror Debts & Double Write-downs

We start with US Bonds. It's an easier process to explain. It also showcases the magnitude of impact on debt reduction – UP TO $5 trillion in Federal Deficits – wiped clean.

US Bonds are the last step in this assembly line of America's mortgage system. It's already passed thru the ***First Group of the Home Mortgage Partners*** as well as the ***Second Group of the Wall Street Partners***.

Much of the debt held by most of the *Partners* are *Mirror Debts*. And..., most *Partners* also took *Double Write-downs* on their *Mirror Debts*. This was done before the gov't took over those assets. *US Bonds* therefore include ALL the *Double Write-downs* from ALL the previous *Partners*

By 2008 - 9, each *Group* had written off a sizable portion of their debts. EX: Banks had written off large portions of their mortgage holdings – both the 1st and 2nd Mortgage and (almost all the) PMI Insurance.

The same again for Wall Street *Partners*. They wrote-off vast amounts of their *Securitized Mortgages* and trillions more in *Credit Default Swaps*.

This gives us a *Double-Write-down* by 5 different *Partners*. These *write-downs* had been completed before the gov't stepped in with their banking bailouts. This means that those *US Bonds* are likely - almost entirely - made of *Phantom Debt*. It doesn't really exist – as we explain shortly. There was but a small fraction of debt left by the time gov't packaged these securities into *US Bonds*.

Now for the fun part:

Chapter 14

Unraveling the Debt Crisis

Lehman Collapse – Paid-off Your Mortgage

Lehman Brothers lost $780 billion in a matter of days. Let's say they carried equal parts *Securitized Mortgages* and *Credit Default Swaps* – about $400 billion each.

Now for the *Double Pay-down*.

A 'Securitized Mortgages' is your home loan repackaged and sold to Wall Street. They added the word 'Securitized' to the name (ironic to say the least). But remember, that's nothing more than a duplicate copy of your home mortgage. It's a *Mirror Debt* of your home loan.

Here's what that means.

Let's say Lehman was holding your $100k home loan as a *Securitized Mortgage*. When they went broke and loss $780 billion, this also retired your $100k home loan. All of it.

In our example from Chapter, your home loan was $100k. *THAT $100K LOAN WAS PAID OFF WITH LEHMAN'S BANKRUPTCY. YOUR NEW MONTHLY HOME MORTGAGE PAYMENT SHOULD HAVE BEEN ONE BIG 0.* You should have been able to go out and refinance the home all over again – at the new market price. The real estate market would have rebounded almost immediately had this been implemented across throughout the system.

Now for the best part. *YOUR HOME MORTGAGE WAS PAID-OFF: AND SO TOO WAS THE DEBT OF EVERY OTHER PARTNER OF THE MORTGAGE SYSTEM.* This is a very, very simple version of the point, but it is an accurate portrayal of it. We will provide the gruesome details for those nerds of interest – later.

The **First Group** of **Partners** had all their debts retired.

Group 1; Home Mortgage: 3 Partners (#1 thru #3)

1) **PAID IN FULL:** Wells Fargo – 1st Mortgage (80% of the loan).
2) **PAID IN FULL:** Chase Manhattan – 2nd Mortgage.
3) **PAID IN FULL:** AIG: - PMI Insurance.

The same was also true for the **Second Group** - Wall Street.

Group 2; Wall Street: 2 Partners (#4 – #5)

4) **PAID IN FULL:** Goldman Sachs – *'Mortgage Backed Securities.'*
5) **WRITE-OFF - IN FULL:** Lehman Brothers – *CDS (Credit Default Swaps)*.

The **Third Group of Partners** - our 401k life savings are the one exception. Our 401k's immediately showed a 100% of those losses on our retirement portfolio. However, this loss would have been fully refunded had the mortgage title been placed with you – as it should have been. Your 401k was the only one, true holder of this mortgage debt. All other parties were working and functioning like brokers only. This is a different discussion for a later Chapter.. Though all this debt was not retired, the write-down to your portfolio had the same impact as Lehman's bankruptcy. It was in fact the very definition of a *Write-down* to the home mortgage.

Group 3; 401 K Grandma's Retirement: 1 Partner (#6)

6) **Write-down**: *Title of Home:* Charles Swab.

This brings us to the **Fourth Group of Partners** - the gov't and their *US Bonds*.

And now for *LEDER's* magic of the *Double Write-down* – next chapter.

Chapter 15

$5 Trillion in US Deficits – Wiped Clean

Tracking Double-Paydowns

Lehman Collapse was the *Double Pay-down*

The collapse of Lehman should have represented a massive debt reduction for the entire system – under *LEDER (Leverage Debt Reduction)*. It removed a mountain of debt – once multiplied by *LEDER*. Instead, this was a time bomb of mass destruction to the global financial system.

We have covered a lot of ground in this book. You have learned about the *7 Partners* and *4 Groups, Mirror Debts* and *Double Paydowns*. Now, we get see how all these different pieces come together. Combined, they would have resolved much of the crisis with relative ease.

We will use our example of the $100k Home Mortgage once more.

Remember Wells Fargo and Chase Manhattan carried the 1st and 2nd Mortgage on your $100k loan.

Chase also had a PMI insurance policy on its 2nd mortgage offered by AIG.

ALL OF THOSE DEBTS HAD JUST BEEN PAID-OFF BY LEHMAN'S COLLAPSE. HOWEVER, NONE OF THE PARTNERS NOTED THIS 'WRITE-DOWN' BY LEHMAN. WELLS FARGO, CHASE AND AIG STILL THOUGHT THEY HELD 100% OF THEIR ORIGINAL DEBT.

A C-DEL (CHRONICLE OF DEBT LEDGERS) WOULD HAVE ALLOWED WELLS FARGO, CHASE AND AIG TO DISCOVER THAT THEIR DEBTS WERE NOW WIPED CLEAN. THEIR SO-CALLED LIABILITY WAS LITTLE MORE THAN 'PHANTOM DEBT.'

Same again for *Group 2* – Goldman Sachs and their Securitized Mortgage. All their debt had just been erased too, but none of that was recorded to their *Mirror Debts*.

Here's what happened instead.

These banks were told (mis-informed) that the value of their mortgage assets had just collapsed by 80%. They would each have to take a 'write-down' of their own. All the Partners were struggling by this time. None could afford to take a 80% write-off. They managed 20% to 50% - instead.

None of them cross-referenced their respective *Mirror Debts* with other *Partners*. Unfortunately, they all believed they were stuck with 'toxic assets.' If only they had known about the 7 Partners, *Mirror Debts* and *Double Write-downs*.

5 Partners w/ 15% Double Write-downs = 75%

Let's say each of these 5 *Partners* had written off 15% of their respective holdings. It means 75% of these securities had already been written off.

Surprising how even a small write-down by each *Partner* adds up into a large reduction. This would have left much of the remaining debt almost entirely paid off by the time these securities were packaged into *US Bonds*.

30% Double Write-downs = 150%

Let's double this and say each *Partner* wrote-off 30% (often, it was much more). That gives us nearly 150% in combined write-downs. These are working figures, but it offers a fair portrayal. Here's what a $150% worth of *Double Write-down* means:

a) 100% of those US Bonds made of these securities were already paid off – long ago.
b) 50% to 100% of all home mortgages (from pre-2008) had also been paid off as well.
c) Much of the remaining real estate securities still left slushing around Wall Street (from 2008) were also paid off - in full.

This gives us some idea on how much **Phantom Debt** we have left in our financial system. It can be retired once all *Double Write-downs* have been consolidated and applied. How? (Next Chapter)

Chapter 16

Tap Trillions in Savings:

Refinance Entire Market

Punchline: How to Tap Savings

We will cover the details of 'how-to' and 'the why' we had so many *Mirror Debts*..Chapter.. We will also point to the host of *Double Paydowns* from the 2008 crisis - onwards. Those details will help map the process for an insurance like service. Such an insurance program would serve a cross section of financial sectors, products and services.

For now, we jump to the punchline. Here's how we can tap the trillions in savings from all the *Double Write-downs* – now – from those already in the system. Trillins in debt - retired over-night.

The simple answer is to refinance all remaining debts carried over from the 2008 mortgage crisis. This would include all mortgages or mortgage backed securities. Do so again for all the *US Bonds* packaged from those Securitized Mortgages.

$5 to $10 Trillion in Refinancing for Banks & Wall Street

The pockets of *Double Paydowns* now buried throughout today's system is hard to pinpoint. It can be consolidated by flushing out the entire system. Refinancing all those old debts would be the easiest and fastest way to tap all those savings.

How we arrive at the total savings from all the *Double Paydowns*? It's a bit technical. It will require a series of simple formulas and a number of steps to demonstrate the entire process. We will cover all this for our dear super-nerds interested in the mechanics of it. For now, we leave you with the punchline and final step to capitalizing on all the savings: Refinance all 2008 debts.

Banks will love this. It means refinancing $5 to $10 trillion in home mortgages, securitized mortgage packages, CDS policies and US Bonds.

We will cover these considerations in just a bit. For now, let's take a detour to a second area of debts that *LEDER* can help 'Deleverage.' There are a number of 'blue-color' industries that also duplicate debts. Construction is a great example. So is manufacturing and retail.

This other brand of debt is called Avatar Loans. Understanding Avatar Loans will help broaden the picture of America's greater value and how much more is just *Phantom Debt*. In other words, the USA has 30% to 60% less debt then we are presently led to believe. Avatar Loans will showcase another sector of such *Phantom Debts*.

Part 2 Main Street

Chapter 17

Avatar Loans:

Leverage Financing in Blue Collar Industries

Avatar Loans

Chapter 1 talked of 'Mirror Debts.' Here we cover *'Avatar Loans.'*

An *Avatar Loan* is where multiple loans are taken out against the same project. Those loans are paid in full upon the projection's completion. *Avatar Loans* are truly separate loans, unlike *Mirror Debts*. However, *Avatar Loans* carry the same kinds of multiplied impact upon debt reduction. *Avatar Loans* is another area that *LEDER (Leverage Debt Reduction)* can work wonders.

Home construction makes for is an easy example of Avatar Loans. We find Avatar Loans with most manufacturing and development projects.

'Mirror Debts' can seem obvious when we talk of financial markets but it may be a surprise to hear that there's something similar in blue collar industries as well. We use the example of a developer to show how *Avatar Loans* works.

Construction: $50k Asset Against $500k Debt

The Developer takes a loan out to buy a $50,000 lot of land and another $200,000 to build a home on it. He now has $250,000 worth of debt.

Contractor $150k Loans

Here's where the *Avatar Loans* begin to multiply.

The Developer hires a contractor. The contractor also takes out a loan. He buys materials and hires subcontractors – plumber, electrician, roofer, tile layer, etc. Let's say the Contractor takes out a loan for $150,000 to cover his construction job.

Sub-Contractors: $60k Loans

Each one of his sub-contractors also take out loans of their own. The plumber buys bathroom and kitchen furnishings. The electrician buys wiring and switches and the same for the roofer, etc. They each go out and buy materials and hire workers to help in their project. Let's say the sub-contractors have taken out another $60,000 in loans between them.

Workers: $35k Loans

All the construction workers hired for the job also go and use their credit cards. They know they have more money coming so they buy things for home and family. Their credit cards total $35,000 in new debt.

Retailers: $55k Loans

Home Depot and other suppliers / retailers have this new wave of buyers. They also go and tap their credit to fill this new inventory demand from the (sub)contractors and workers. Let's say Home Depot and the retailers use $55,000 of credit.

Bank: $250,000

Let's not forget about the bank that loaned to the Developer. That is another $250,000 *Avatar Loan*.

AVATAR Loans Total: $800,000

Once we add up all those different loans, we end up with $800k in Avatar Loans.

Bank	$	250,000
Developer	$	250,000
Contractor	$	150,000
Sub-Contractors	$	60,000
Workers	$	35,000
Home Depot	$	55,000
Total	$	800,000

The loans taken by each of these Partners is referred to as an *Avatar Loan*. We now have $800k worth of *Avatar Loans*.

These are not '*Mirror Loans*.' They are not a duplicate debt like we saw of the student loan (co-signed by mom and dad) Chapter 1. *Avatar Loans* are separate loans, however, each of them is based upon the same (construction) project. They are all paid off once that project - house - is completed.

Understanding *Avatar Loans* will help identify the hidden values laying behind today's mountains of debt. That is true for a host of industries from manufacturing and product development; to retailing and even marketing. Tracking *Avatar Loans* will help identify the central asset behind all the debts. We can then resize these debts into manageable tasks like we saw of the house construction. Each Partner carried a reasonable amount of debt compared to the profit they stood to make from their job.

Avatar Loans give us a new tool set to pinpoint which step of the construction process offer a fair return compared to those areas that are overpriced.

Chapter 18

Untangle Hidden Values Behind Debt

Total Debt = $500k vs $50k Asset

The last chapter gave the example of a construction project. The developer went out and took a $250k loan and hired sub-contractors to do the work. The example has a $250,000 construction project against $800,000 worth of (Avatar) loans.

$800k is the total once we add up all the different loans taken out by all the different (sub) contractors working on building that home.

Let's bring back the investment *'Expert'* we talked about in Chapter 1. The *Expert* again looks over all these different loans. He sees 800k worth of debt. The only hard asset backing any of it is the original $50k worth of land.

The *Expert* sees 16 x more debt than the land is worth. The *Expert* fails to see the link between these debts and all the different Partners to the construction process. Of course, the entire $800k worth of *Avatar Loans* are all related to the same housing project. Completing this home construction resolves that $800k debt. The *Expert* misses this connection. In other words, completing the project will fold that $800k debt into a $350k new home asset.

That seemingly massive $800k worth of debt shrinks to just $250k once the house is completed. All the contractors are paid – at a profit. The same again for the workers and retailers. Let's say all the parties walked off with a combined profit of $75k. That $800k translated into a 15% profit – plus the house.

Much of this talk of debt by today's experts are once again primarily in these *Mirror Debts* and *Avatar Loans*. *LEDER (Leverage Debt Reduction)* is the toolset to help untangle the confusion and find all the true values to be tapped.

Compare this against all those Experts insisting that this debt can never be paid-off. How could $800k worth of debt ever be paid off by one piece of land worth just $50k? This offers a rough idea to the narrative we get from today's *Experts* in contrast to the actual value to be found. It seems to be an impossible mountain of debt. *Avatar Loans, Mirror Debts and Double Paydowns* will help us clarify such misreading and so begin the process of untangling and tapping all the hidden values throughout America's credit/debt system.

Chapter 19

VALDOS vs LIDOS:

Value-Debts vs Liability Debts

Raghu-nomics looks for the (prospective) value and (potential) hard assets behind all the mountains of debt. Raghu-nomics is based upon this simple approach. We are finding a treasure trove of hidden values behind a host of seemingly unrelated debts much like we saw of *Avatar Loans* and *Mirror Debts*. Today's system lacks the insight and mechanism to identify and track these varying values and debt reduction prospects. Here's a rough idea how we do it when it comes to *Avatar Loans*.

Let's take the example of the Developer once again. He took $250k loan to build his house and hired (sub)contractors to build it. The contractors took out loans for a combined total of $800k. All of those loans were based on just the $50k worth of land and the house that WAS GOING TO BE built upon it. This is where *VALDOS* come into play.

VALDOS: Value-Debts-of-Outcome –

($500k Debt Converts to $350k Asset)

Let's say that this $50k land is now worth $350,000 once the house is completed. That $800k debt converts into a home with a 30% equity. We refer to this $800k debt as a ***Value-Debts-of-Outcome*** or ***VALDOS***. This means the Debt has a net Value once the Outcome (transaction) is completed.

In this example, we are giving the house a $350k market value. That $800k of construction debt now CONVERTS into a $350k asset – once the house is completed. This real estate deal has a debt of $250k with a $100k worth of surplus value - a 30% equity.

LIDOS: Liability-Debts-of-Outcome

We only get this new home equity if the house construction is completed. If the house is not finished, we really do have $800k worth of debts. That debt remains a complete liability. We refer to that debt as *'Liability-Debts-of-Outcome*: *LIDOS.'*

VALDOS vs LIDOS: Market Stabilizer

The difference between this $350k asset (*VALDO*) versus a $800k in liability (*LIDOS*) is whether the home construction is completed.

The primary problem with today's financial system is that there is no process to sort the $800k *VALDOS* from the $800k *LIDOS*. The net result is that minor market shifts can convert all debts to now appear to be *LIDOS*. This would then alter all values into 16 x more debt than there are in assets. The *Experts* insisting we are a market of *LIDOS* will of course crash investor sentiment and so becomes a self-fulfilling prophecy. A system for tracking all aspects of such projects will help remove the hype of destruction that goes to the center of the very worst in our financial system.

This is the story behind the 2008 market meltdown. By our rough calculations, there was 70% to 80% in *VALDOS*. The market reaction was that there 90% *LIDOS* - exact opposite of our calculations.

We are once again beginning to hear much the same from today's *Experts*. They are talking about all the debts and how it runs many times more the nations GNP. Much of this is like looking at the credit reports of each contractor, supplier and worker as unrelated debt. Such a report misses the common value. Therefore, they can't recognize that a good portion of that debt would fold into an asset with a surplus value like we see of our house - once construction is completed.

Today's experts can't find the values behind all today's debt obligations. The primary danger to today's financial system is this inability to identify all the prospective values and see how close we are to tapping them. We calculate that there is a 40% to 60% *VALDOS* in today's market. We therefore gather we need only find 20% to 40% more value to bridge us to an 80% threshold of value against liability. A market can absorb a 20% correction. First on our list: small biz. More on that later.

Chapter 20

More Tools for More Market Bubbles

Solution to Coming Implosion: RADHA Mortgage

Leverage Debt Reduction holds the key to retiring trillions in debt. Resolving today's debt crisis may prove far easier than most think possible. However, the last market implosion had far less debt - and a lot more value to fall back upon by compare. For example, today's *Credit Default Swap* market is just half those of 2008. They provided a significant buffer of capital to fall back on (though the *Experts* thought it represented more liability rather than less). This is just one of several examples to the added resources missing from today's system to dealing with any coming market slowdowns. Therefore, covering the coming implosion will require more than just *Leverage Debt Reduction* alone. We have a number of other programs being developed for this to complement our efforts of reducing debt and building added value.

For example, we developed a new mortgage product. It's called the RADHA Mortgage. The RADHA Mortgage pays down over inflated real estate – starting at 20%, but with 50% being an average - while building equity far faster than any other mortgage systems.

The RADHA Mortgage was first conceived during Japan's 1990's real estate market crash. The idea was resurrected in response to America's market crash of 2008. We were trying to understand the value-added-system of the RADHA Mortgage. We ended up discovering all these other goldmines like *Leverage Debt Reduction, Double-Paydowns and Mirror Loans*.

We have other programs like the 'Inflation Tax' that re-balances over inflated real estate markets.

'America's New Deal 2' does much the same for over-inflated stock markets.

American Shopping Party does the same for small biz.

These programs will be covered in other books. For now, we start here with *Leverage Debt Reduction*. Each of these programs all work from the same principle – find related players and layers of values. Combine them to reduce the liability to each and multiply their efforts and values for all.

We introduce the concept behind these templates. It's our call to action to other nerds. Put on your engineering caps. Let's get a jumpstart on this coming economic tsunami. *Leverage Debt Reduction* is geared to build out a new toolset for taking on the coming market shake-up.

This rough draft represents the first 1/3 of the book once completed. Another third will cover more details on both the reasons and steps to the 'dismemberment of our mortgage assets.' For example, mortgages divided-up into 'tranches' based upon the year (1st year, 2n year, etc.). This division goes to the heart of the mess in tracking mortgages to securities, etc. Blockchain to the rescue of course.

The final third will provide variety of ways to identify and build out new values. For example, *CDS (Credit Default Swaps)* had a premium charge that ranged from 0.5% to 3% (10% for Greece) against the total of the Securitized package the investor bought. We averaged those differences into 1.5% premium, but remember, there was 5 such *CDS* for every home mortgage in America. That means there was the equivalent of 7.5% in *CDS* premiums being paid per year – PER YEAR.

If there was an average of 5 years per *CDS* policy, we are looking at a total of 37% worth of premiums that had already been paid on *CDS* policies as a whole by 2008. We are looking at nearly 40% in *Double Write-downs* in just 1 area of *Mirror Debts*. By 2008, the *CDS* market alone actually could have covered the entire market Write-downs. This is before any of the other Mirror Debt Partners would have had to make a single Paydown. More details to this, but these kinds of details will be covered in the 3rd part of the book.

LEDER (Leverage Debt Reduction) will reset the context of our entire financial system with a great deal more value, less debt and a sense of confidence in both the added supports behind it and all the new prospects and untapped values to be found in it - worth trillions.

To be Re-written and Misc. Notes

Chapter 21

3 Home Mortgage Partners

Mortgage Partners vs Wall Street Partners

We finally arrive at our working model. Here's how this process could have been applied to the 2008 market crash. It begins with the first Group – the Partners in the Home Mortgage.

Mortgage Partners

A typical home mortgage comes in two parts.

The first *Partner* is the 1st mortgage holder.

The other 5 *Partners* are involved with the 2nd Mortgage.

1st Mortgage - covers the first 80% of the home's value. (*Partner* 1)

2nd Mortgage - covers remaining 20% of the home mortgage. (*Partner* 2)

Banks often specialize in just one of these two markets.

Wells Fargo focused on the 1st Mortgage - back in 2008 (if I remember correctly). I know Chase Manhattan specialized in 2nd Mortgages.

1st and 2nd Mortgage Players: Wells Fargo & Chase

Let's use the example of a $100,000 home.

The first mortgage covers 80% = $80,000.

The second mortgage covers the last 20% = $20,000.

Let's say you default and stop making payments to your mortgage. The Second Mortgage holder (Chase Manhattan) takes the loss on the first $20,000.

Let's say the property value falls 25%. The 1st Mortgage holder – Wells Fargo - would write-off (just) 5%. The 2nd Mortgage holder – Chase - covers the rest – the remaining 20%.

PMI Insurance for 2nd Mortgage - 3rd Mirror Debt: AIG

PMI is an insurance policy that covers the 2nd mortgage. This PMI is an insurance policy for Chase Manhattan. PMI Insurance would cover the entire $20k of the 2nd mortgage – for Chase.

PMI reimburses Chase Manhattan against any loses to that 2nd mortgage. AIG may have been the provider for PMI Insurance in 2008.

This gives us 3 partners to that home mortgage.

1) Wells Fargo – 1st Mortgage (80% of the loan).
2) Chase Manhattan – 2nd Mortgage. (Covers the first 20% of losses).
3) AIG: - Insures 2nd mortgage for Chase against 100% of any losses.

Here we see how each step of the system has the partner serve as a back-up to the one before them. This back-up is now duplicated further by Wall Street –next chapter.

Chapter 22

3 Wall Street Partners

There are 6 Partners. Here, we focus on the 2nd mortgage. The 2nd Mortgage has a total of 4 partners – two from the home mortgage side. Ttwo from Wall Street. Here's the Wall Street side.

(The last chapter introduced the first 3 Partners of the first Group. Those Partners work with the homeowner's mortgage. That mortgage is then handed over to Wall Street. Wall Street is the 2nd group of the mortgage system. They come with two *Partners* of their own. Wall Street duplicates the same steps for investors that we saw for the home mortgage and PMI insurance.)

Mortgage Backed Securities – 4th Mirror Debt: Goldman Sachs

We now introduce the fourth *Mirror Debt*. It's handled by the *Second Group*. This is the 3rd *Partner* in the assembly line of this mortgage journey.

Is this starting to seem a bit convoluted? Confusing? You're not alone. This is where the whole system begins to break down. It's at this step that we lose track of the mortgage. No surprise it happens where Wall Street steps in. They packaged this into '*Mortgage Backed Securities*.' Those mortgages were bundled together and sold to investors.

Goldman Sachs was one of the more notorious traders of those 'investments.'

Credit Default Swaps – 5th Mirror Debt: Lehman Brothers

There remains one additional insurance policy to this 2nd Mortgage. Investors had an insurance policy for their '*Mortgage Backed Securities.*' That insurance program was called a *Credit Default Swap – CDS*. This covered investors against a home buyer who defaulted on their mortgage (among other market risks). The investor is paid by their *CDS* policy against losses to their '*Securitized Mortgage.*'

Lehman Brothers traded *CDS* policies. They are the 4th partner on the 2nd Home Mortgage.

We have now identified the 5 *Partners* on the 1st and 2nd mortgage and their respective *Mirror Debts*. We will cover the gov't after the role of these first 5 Partners have been covered.

Group 1; Home Mortgage – 3 Partners

1) Wells Fargo – 1st Mortgage (80% of the loan).
2) Chase Manhattan – 2nd Mortgage. (Covers the first 20% of losses).
3) AIG: - Insures 2nd mortgage for Chase against 100% of any losses.

Group 2; Wall Street – 2 Partners

4) Goldman Sachs – '*Mortgage Backed Securities*' (Securitized Mortgages) investment packages.
5) Lehman Brothers – *CDS* (Credit Default Swaps) Insurance Policy on those Securitize Mortgage packages.

Group 3; Gov't Bail-outs

6) Federal Reserve & US Treasury – Quantitative Easing, etc

Chapter 21

Split Costs 4 ways = Capital Market Insurance

Join Forces: "Pairing," "Partners"

The last two chapters identified the 5 different Partners of a home mortgage – **Mirror Debt Holders.** 4 of them are **Partners** on the 2nd Mortgage.

Normally, each **Partner** functions as they do now - without cross **Pairing** each other's capital pool, practices and payments. However, once the market begins to slide, these 4 parties should be ready to join forces. Or rather, the **Secondary Insurer Provider** would coordinate them.

The process of 'grouping' (all the **'Counter-Partners'** of *Mirror Debts)* is called **'Pairing'** or **'Paired.'**

Split Cost 4 Ways

We now have 4 *Partners* to the homes 2nd Mortgage.

Partner 1: Chase Manhattan Bank: They provide the 2nd mortgage.

Partner 2: AIG: They offer PMI Insurance on the 2nd mortgage.

Partner 3: Goldman Sachs: They specialized in *Mortgage Backed Securities and sold that mortgage as a security.*

Partner 4: Lehman Brothers: They insured the *Mortgage Security for Goldman Sachs.* The policies were called *CDS (Credit Default Swaps).*

'Pairing' = 'Capital Market Insurance'

LEDER –(*Leverage Debt Reduction*) has each *Partner* cover a portion of the 2nd Mortgage – once written down. This makes it affordable for each of them.

We continue with the example of the $100k home from Chapter 8. The 2nd Mortgage is $20k. That is split between each of the 4 *Partners*.

Chase Manhattan writes-offs $5,000.

AIG writes-off another $5,000.

Goldman Sachs writes-off $5,000.

Lehman - $5,000

Each of these Partners had been paying/receiving income from their respective program. They often received an income for years – (half) decade. They would now pay from that earned income.

Lehman for example had 5 *CDS* policies. They had been receiving a premium payment for each one of their (insurance) *CDS* policies - for years. We cover the capital pool that provided to them – Chapter 20. It demonstrates just how much capital had been available to use for this kind of market loss. Lehman may have received more income than the other Partners. It may therefore prove more affordable to have them cover a larger share than the others. How much each Partner should pay can change, but the general principle of a shared cost remains.

This is also shows the important of having this program ready before markets dive once again. The **C-DELS** (*Chronicles of Debt Ledgers*) should be *Paired* and ready to go. It's like any insurance. You buy it before a disaster.

This working model is fairly simple. We are applying the principles of insurance: Pool capital from multiple parties to cover the cost for when they face a disaster. This makes it so much more affordable for all of them.

Welcome to "*Capital Market Insurance.*"

Chapter 21

Write-down on 1% vs 75% Loss

1% the Costs of the Market vs 80%

The last chapter showed how we could cut losses by 75% - to each **Partner** of the 2nd mortgage. We *'Paired' Partners* with other *Mirror Debt* **'Holders.'** They pooled their resources and divided losses between them. Each *Partner* paid just a quarter the costs.

That's a simplified version of the savings. The actual savings are far greater. It would have reduced loss to just 1.5% of the markets total value. Compare that to 85% loss we saw of 2008.

Here's how it would work:

a) America's total real estate market in 2007 was valued at about $12 trillion.

b) 20% of that market was facing foreclosures by 2008. That comes to $2.4 trillion. The remaining $9.5 trillion (80%) of the market was still holding its value by 2008.

c) Home prices dropped 20% in their respective local markets. Let's say it was Detroit, Los Angeles and Dallas. They lost 20% of their value. The homes could still be re-sold for 80% their original value. However, the rest of the country had not yet been affected. They still held 100% of their value.

d) The total value lost was still under 20%. That SHOULD have been covered by Chase Manhattan as the 2nd Mortgae holder. The 1st Mortgage holder – Wells Fargo – should have been saved from any losses. Under **LEDER** (Leverage Debt Reduction), they would not have had any losses that year.

e) Here's where it gets interesting. There was a 20% loss on the home prices. BUT, that was true for just 20% of America's housing market. The other 80% of the market had not been affected yet. In other words, it was 20% of 20%. That equals just 5% of the market. We only needed to pay-off 5% of the market by 2008.

f) 2008 was ground zero for the market crash. And yet, 5% would have been enough to have covered all market losses by that time.

g) That 5% is split 4 ways by *LEDER*. That runs about 1.5% the total market to be paid by each Partner. Compare this to the 85% paid-out - covered next - Chapter 11.

1% vs 85%. Welcome to *LEDER: Leverage Debt Reduction*.

Chapter 22

Loss: $70 Billion vs $780 Billion

Step 1: $120 Billion

The last chapter showed that **LEDER** - *Leverage Debt Reduction* - would have reduced the cost / loss to each Partner to just 1.5% the markets total value.

The last chapter explained how we only needed to pay down 5% - not the 85% we saw of 2008.

a) 5% comes to $480 billion by 2008.
b) This $480 billion is $120 billion per industry player:
    i)   Chase Manhattan – 2nd Mortgage,
    ii)   AIG – PMI Insurance,
    iii)   Goldman Sachs – Securitized Mortgages
    iv)   Lehman Brother's – Credit Default Swaps: CDS.

Each **Partner** would pay this $120 billion – write-down. Remember, this only impacted the 2nd Mortgage industry. The total market melt-down was under that first 20%. That is covered by the 2nd mortgage. The 1st Mortgage holders – Wells Fargo - would still have been entirely untouched.

We would have recommended a small gov't bail-out at this juncture. This makes it very affordable to everyone – including the gov't. They are the back-up to the '**Secondary Market Provider**.' A gov't contribution would reduce the total to just $70 billion per *Partner*.

Compare this to Lehman Brothers 85% loss in 2008. The company went from a value of $800 billion to just $20 billion - in about 2 weeks. That was their selling price about a month later in 2008. (More on that in Chapter 16.)

Lehman Brothers was the trigger to the entire market implosion *LEDER (Leverage Debt Reduction)* would have kept Lehman Brothers solvent. The cost to Lehman –$70 billion vs the $780 they ended up losing.

Chapter 23

Gov't Bail-out: $200 Billion vs $5 Trillion

Gov't $200 Billion vs $5 Trillion

We showed how much gov't would have saved with **LEDER** *(Leverage Debt Reduction)*. The **Partners** of the home mortgage could have covered the cost under *LEDER* at this stage of the market crash. However, there was still more market correction to follow. We would therefore have recommended the gov't to step in to reassure markets.

An ideal amount would have been about 20%. That would be $200 billion. That would reduce the cost to all the other partners to $70 billion from $120 billion.

The gov't was blackmailed by Wall Street to come in with an immediate $1 trillion bail-out. This was follow-ed with another $5 trillion in 'Quantitative Easing' – another gov't bailout. The gov't purchased those 'bad debts.' LEDER would have costs maybe 10% that amount or $500 billion.

This is the function Leverage Debt Reduction can offer. It will resize market bubbles with smaller liabilities and greater value. Market bubbles are building throughout a number of industries today. Later chapters provide some details how this would have played out for the 2008 market. The basic mechanism is rather simple.

The world faces a new and much larger 'market correction' then we saw of 2008. Leverage Debt Reduction can help sidestep much of this coming collapse. However, this Mirror Debt tracking system (aka Chronicles of Debt Ledgers: C-Dels) needs to be implemented before markets tank. Once markets implode, it's much harder to re-assemble the original value.

Think of our example of the $50k student loan. Once in default, it impairs the credit rating of both parents that co-signed for it. The harm is multiplied far beyond you and your original student loan. It impacts all the debts and credit ability of your mom and dad as well.

Market implosions do much the same. The bad debt destroys the remaining 'real' market values along with it. Leverage Debt Reduction would have cost just a fraction of the nearly $20 trillion in market losses we saw of the 2008 collapse or the $2 ($5) trillion in gov't bail-outs. Put another way: Leverage Debt Reduction is the ounce of prevention to the 10,000 pounds of cure.

The process of Leverage Debt Reduction is 'De-Leveraging Debt.'

(Gov't saved banks from those losses by buying those 'troubled assets.' The loss was to our 401ks. Many savings accounts loss 50% or more.)

We will explain how and why in the later chapters. For now, we want to point to another market that also carries something similar to *Mirror Debts*. They are called *Avatar Loans*. That's next.

Chapter 24

Today's Expert:

3 x the Debt; 1/3rd the Value

Mirror Debts and *Phantom Debts* are all part of this new tool set by *Leverage Debt Reduction*. These tools resize debts into much smaller amounts and reset the market values much higher.

Let's take the example of your student loan (yes again) (Chapter 1). The total debt went from $150k to just $50k - once we traced the *'Ledger'* back to its original source - you. Tracing the loan back to you showed us the *Experts* 'accounting mistake.'

Our example also showed how your $20k loan payment slashed the remaining balance down to $30k, not the $90k - as the *Expert* thought.

This $30k is divided between 3 people – you and your two parents. That leaves just $10k per person. It's not $30k each - as the *Expert* also thought.

The *Experts* got it wrong at each step of the process. He grossly over-estimated the liabilities to each party. He inflated the remaining debt 3 fold and misdiagnosed the true financial status of your accounts.

This example gives some idea how far *Experts* distorted the market's true status. They paint a picture wildly off mark of the true value.

By contrast, Leverage Debt Reduction will reduce the amount of total debt listed on 'the books' while finding new values to be gained from it.

Chapter 25

Phantom Debt vs Greatest Value

Phantom Debt

Today's system makes it easy to track payments on a co-signed student loan. There is no such system to track all the *Mirror Debts* for industries like **CDS** (*Credit Default Swaps*). Missing this critical step creates a massive façade of **'Phantom-Debt.'**

Much of this so-called debt does not exist. In the case of 2008, it left us with the appearance of tens of trillions in *Phantom Debt*. Most of that so-called debt did not actually exist.

It's just like that $50k student loan mentioned in Chapter 1. The *'Expert'* thought there was $150k worth of debts. He was wrong. There was the original $50k student loan - only. That same loan was simply reflected in each of your family's 3 accounts (once your parents co-signed the loan for you). Each of you served as a back-up - guarantor - for that loan.

There's one difference between your parents as co-signers and Wall Street's *Mirror Debts*. Wall Street paid on each of their respective debts. It would be like your parents paying on your student loan the same time you are. It pays down the debt so much faster. Once again, the problem: None of those payments were tracked and registered to their counter-part *Mirror Debts*.

The net result is obvious. *Phantom Debt* creates massive market distortions. It gives the impression we have far more debt than what actually exist. **LEDER** *(Leverage Debt Reduction)* cuts through the confusion. This allows us to find a host of hidden values now buried by *Experts* and all their distortion. The *10 Mirror Debts* of the last chapter captures the point. It gives some hint to all the value just waiting to be discovered.

The 10 'Liabilities' Offered Greatest Value

Take the 'Experts' of 2008. They pointed to the 10 *Mirror Debts* as one, big liability. (Chapter 6) They screamed about the $65 trillion in *Credit Defaults Swaps*. They did the same again about *Securitized Mortgages*. They pointed to the $13 trillion in real estate mortgages. They insisted America faced all sorts of market bubbles. Their estimates ran $100 trillion in market debts and liabilities - bubbles.

What a dreadful (mis)*Reading* of the market. Each one of those industries were a duplication of the same debt – your home mortgage. Put another way, all those different *Mirror Debts* represented the markets greatest value.

Each *Mirror Debt* was a re-re-re-re-re-re insurance policy (of sorts) to America's real estate. This offered us the most insured financial / real estate markets in history.

That $100 trillion represented various back-ups to support America's $12 trillion real estate market. 9 fold in back-ups. The *Experts* were entirely blind to the value this offered us. Therefore, they could never tap the host of treasures laying there to be discovered. A *Secondary Insurance* service is only one of many examples to the kinds of opportunities to be found.

Chapter 26

China – Contrast

Phantom Debt

China offers a good contrast. Compare America's real estate crisis to China's prospects. They face a real estate bubble of their own. I gather much of it was not packaged into securities. Nor do they have the *CDS* market to insure those secureities. I wonder if they have a 2nd mortgage holder for their properties. How about PMI insurance? They have far fewer partners to their housing market. Who do they have to call upon when their housing market goes bust?

In contrast, America shared the debt reduction with a host of different players in their bailout program – as an example. China has no such partnerships to call upon. They stand alone. No back-ups. They could only wish to have 9 back-ups to support them. This may face a greater economic slow down than the USA did in 2008 – even though it is less debt.

America had 10 partners. Each was paying on their respective policy/debt. We only needed to consolidate their combined contributions. This would have covered the cost of the real estate market correction.

The Next chapter offers us a working model how this could have worked.

Chapter 27

Combining 10 *Mirror Debts*

Conspiracies w Positive Results

The last chapter outlined the 10 different partners to the home mortgage. Each was paying on their respective **Mirror Debts**. These 10 *Mirror Debts* gives us some idea how much back-up had been built into the system by 2008.

The next step seems obvious. All those different revenue streams could be combined to help cover costs. Taken together, they could cover much of it. This kind of coordination is the function of an insurance program.

Wall Street kept sub-dividing real estate mortgages into ever smaller parts or under new headings – Securitized Mortgages, Credit Default Swaps, 1st or 2nd Mortgage, PMI, etc. Critics say all this is just so they can charge more fees. They saw it as one big scam. It may have been the work of devious minds and sheer greed, but the net result gave us a unique set of advantages.

Splicing and dicing mortgages gave us more 'co-signers' to the same mortgage. It gained an ever-growing number of back-ups to the system. It multiplied the number of *Mirror Debts* - and the *Double Paydowns* along with it. The one true blunder was failing to recognize these advantages and tap them.

8 Mirror Debts to Pay 2

In theory, paying-off one (of the 5) *Credit Default Defaults* 'should' have paid-off the other 8 *Mirror Debts* as well. And visa versa. It's more complicated than this, but the point remains. For example, it would have likely taken 8 or 9 (of the 10) *Mirror Debts* to pay-off the other 1 or 2. Details will vary, but the principle of this process offers a fair explanation how *LEDER* could have resolved the market meltdown in 2008 – Chapter 9.

Chapter 28

8 x the Liability

Phantom Debt also hides away vast value. That value can be tapped once identified. Leverage Debt Reduction helps uncover such hidden values – explained in later chapters.

Chapter 29

Credit Default Swaps:

How It Works with Leverage Debt Reduction

'Double Write-down'

Let's say our a Wall Street report talking about $150,000 in Credit Default Swaps. It's really just $50,000 worth of debt counted 3 times – like we saw of our example of the student loan given in the last chapter. In 2008, Credit Default Swaps were counted more than just 3 times, but 5 times. (It's about 2 ½ times today.) Here's our point: Paying off just one of those Credit Default Defaults also pays-off the other 4 'mirror' Credit Default Swaps. We call this a 'Double Write-down.' Welcome to Leverage Debt Reduction.

Credit Default Swap – Insurance Policy on Mortgage

A Credit Default Swap is an insurance policy for investors that buy home mortgages. If the homeowner defaults, the investor is reimbursed the difference by the Credit Default policy. There was 5 insurance policies – Credit Default Swaps - for every home mortgage in America (back in 2008).

This means that each home mortgage 'written-off' by banks also paid-off 5 Credit Default Swaps.

The same is true of Credit Default Swaps. Paying off one Credit Defaults paid off the other 4 'mirror' Credit Default Swaps too. It also paid off the home mortgage as well. It's like the example of the school loan. Pay $20k on the $50k student loan and you just paid off $90k worth from

It's more involved than this, but this is a rough idea of how a 'double paydown' works. We refer to it when talking about the great market meltdown of 2008.

Introducing this double paydown or 'Leverage Debt-Reduction' would have averted the market implosion while also dramatically boosting the value across a great many assets from real estate, mortgages, insurance, 401k, etc.

Leverage Debt Reduction does not require an extra step of cash infusion. It's already part of the process wherein one pays off their area of debt, the reduction shows up in other debt obligations.

This how the market already works. All that is missing is the mechanism to

We are simply suggesting that we need but follow each of those duplicate mirror debts. We can then more easily erase the seemingly impossible debts that face the country.

The market is in dire need for a system that can track how one write-down automatically reduces the obligations across other platforms. Put simply: we need a secondary market player to track and coordinate the retail players for markets like Credit Default Swaps. This will stabilize the over-all market while uncovering these large pockets of hidden value and so unleash trillions in new market prospects.

This was the missing step that would have saved us from the 2007 – 10 real estate meltdown. 'Leverage Debt Reduction' would have found trillions worth of duplicate write-downs throughout a number of markets from real estate, derivatives, insurance, banking and other investments.

Welcome to Leverage Debt Reduction.

Inverse of Leverage Financing

Most people have heard of Leverage Financing. It uses the same one dollar multiple times to make different investments. For example: 1 dollar may finance $5 dollars' worth of investments. This same principle also works in reverse. $1 dollar in repayment can, in turn, pay-off $5 worth of debt obligation.

It happens when we look to unwind (pay-down) 'Leveraged Investments.' Each step of repayment on one debt also writes-down other debts along with it. So, paying $1 of debt in turn also pays-off $5 worth of total debt. Today's system has a number of areas where this proves true. We are proposing a new service that would track this for these different markets – starting with Credit Default Swaps.

Secondary Market for Derivatives & Credit Default Swaps

Warren Buffet is the insurance provider to retail insurance companies. He insures today's insurance companies from default. They may find themselves overwhelmed by some new natural disaster. It could be a hurricane in the Gulf of Mexico; a flood in the Mid-West or fires and earthquake on the West Cost. It cost billions that insurance companies may fail to have on hand. Warren Buffets steps in to carry them through. He is their financial backstop. Behind Warren Buffet stands the Federal gov't. Warren Buffet has greatly reduced how often the Feds have to step-in to save the insurance industry.

This secondary insurance market has stabilized the insurance industry as a whole. Without these secondary insurance players, the entire industry would be more volatile – if not implode. It also serves to buffer continuous governor bailouts.

Having this kind of 'secondary market' player for other markets like Credit Default Swaps would offer a similar kind of financial buffer and stability. Our focus was on the real estate market collapse of 2007 – 2010. We know this to be true for Credit Default Swaps - CDS.

At their most basic, CDS are just another insurance policy. Investors use them against risk to their portfolios. CDS are portrayed as the secondary insurance provider to investors, but they are not. They are actually the RETAIL insurance player much like flood or earth quake insurance companies. Those insurance companies need a secondary insurance service. CDS also need to have their secondary market insurance players as well.

This new secondary insurance service would do for the CDS market as Warren Buffet is doing for today's other insurance companies. The caveat – this market will have a much more active and likely prove a much bigger then today's secondary insurance market. The first player to enter this market will likely prove its prime player. The same holds true for any number of other areas like derivative products.

Credit Default Swaps – 5 Fold Paydown w/ Each Payment

Few things offer a better example of this process than the 2007-9 real estate crisis. It's personified by Credit Default Swaps: a.k.a **CDS**.

The CDS works like an insurance policy. It's taken out by investors when they bought mortgage back securities. Should the value of their mortgage holdings drop; they would be refunded by these CDS policies.

There was $65 trillion in Credit Defaults Swaps (**CDS**) against $12 trillion worth of real estate. That works out to 5 (five) CDS policies for every home mortgage in America.

(This means that paying off just one CDS would in theory pay off the other 4 CDS as well as the home mortgage for which it was issued against. This is what we would refer to as a 'Double-write Down.' More on that later.)

Tranches Multiplied CDS Coverage

These securities were traded lots of times. One reason is that each mortgage was often subdivided into lots of different tranches. For example, the first 1 year of the mortgage would be placed into one tranche. The 2nd to 5th years would be placed into another tranche, etc. Each one of these packages (tranches) would generally have a CDS policy. This is one of several reasons why each home mortgage ended up with a half dozen CDS policies.

Here's where things get really interesting.

7.5% CDS Revenue Per Year, Per Mortgage Security

These CDS policies would cost 0.5% to as much as 5% against the gross value of the investment. (Greece CDS were charging up to 10%.) Let's say the average payment for CDS was 1.5%. This premium was paid annually by the investor.

If you bought $100 worth of mortgage securities, you would pay $1.50 fee for your CDS insurance policy. And remember, there was the equivalent of 5 (five) of these CDS for every home mortgage.

This gives us 1.5% in CDS payments x (times) 5 CDS per year. All told, the CDS insurance market was generating about 7.5% a year in revenues against every home mortgage in America. After 3 to 5 years of paying on these CDS; investors paid the equivalent of 23% (in 3 years) to as much as (nearly) 40% (in 5 years) in CDS insurance coverage.

Securities Dropped 95% while Real Estate Market Fell just 20%

Here's the punchline, the real estate market had only dropped by about 20% in 2008. That 20% drop was only for about 30% to 40% of the total real estate market. That means premiums for CDS was now double the total lost value on the mortgage (market). Put simply, this CDS system actually had enough capital back-up to resolve much of the crisis (without much gov't intervention). The problem was that there was no 'secondary market' player to serve in that role. The insurance industry is a great example.

Secondary Market Player for CDS

Warren Buffet's company insures the insurance companies. Imagine what would happen if the insurance industry did not have this secondary market insurer. The gov't would have to bail the insurance companies a lot more often and for a lot more money. This is what we have with the CDS market today. CDS needed (needs) this same kind of commercial secondary insurer. It would have then worked as effectively as the insurance industry does today. Yes, there would still be some cases where the gov't would need to rescue the secondary market, but it would cost much less and happen far less often.

Leverage Debt Reduction is proposing a company that would serve in this same capacity as Warren Buffet does for the insurance industry. It would be a new industry sector and would complete the process for the CDS market. It is the counter-part and natural stabilizing force to leveraged financing.

In the case of the 2007-8 market, such insight would have allowed an investment firm an incredible advantage. They could have purchased both the mortgages securities (that were selling at 50% to 35% pennies on the dollar) as well as the CDS portfolio's (that were going for as little as just 5% their original value).

The actual real estate market value had only fallen by 20%, but no one could tell if their own portfolio contained those mortgages with this 20% loss. This left everyone dumping their entire securities portfolio. Securities collapsed 50% to 95% though the real estate market itself had fallen only 20% to 30% by then. The industry as a whole held much less loss then their securities and CDS counter parts were trading at.

A Warren Buffet like player in the CDS market could have cashed in on the price difference between those securities and the true real estate market value. The easy way to have done so was simply refinance all the homes at their market value and so cashing out the added value to its securities. This is a simplified version of how it works, but it gives you some idea how big the opportunity would have been. Such a company could have made trillions.

(PMI Insurance makes it 7 areas of paydown.)

Lehman Brothers – Double Paydown

There were other values besides securities selling for much less than the actual real estate itself. One was in the straight forward write-off.

A great example was the collapse of Lehman Brothers. They went from $800 billion to just $20 billion in about 3 weeks. Put another way, that 'write-down' was actually paying off $780 billion in debt obligations on both the CDS market as well as home mortgages.

Most other banks made hefty write-downs as well. Those write downs were also going for 50% to 80% off the original price of their securities holdings. By 2009, securities had been written off by as much as 80% while the market value of the homes they backed had only lost 30%. Homes were still holding at 70% their original value. That's a 50% price difference between the CDS and home prices.

And then we have the 'Double Write-downs' as mentioned above and in our video.

The Warren Buffet of Investments

This gives you some idea to the scope of opportunity for a company using this Raghu-nomics market insight. That is what Leverage Debt Reduction was offering America's real estate market then. It's what we can do for China's real estate market today – or any over-heated market. It would allow China to sidestep their coming real estate bubble (which is about to pop soon).

If a large investment firm built out this Leverage Debt Reduction program, it would position them as the primary clearing house for the entire CDS industry. Another words, they would be for investments as Warren Buffet is for the insurance industry.

That starts with the CDS market for mortgage backed securities (and the host of other market investments as well). I've been looking to connect with a foundation or investment firm that would be interested in building out this program.

Leverage Debt Reduction is the financial 'quantum entanglement' of debt. This offers the same kind of exponential right-down of debt much as Leverage Financing multiplies investment purchasing power. This has all the makings of a new industry. It should prove as large as its counterpart in Leveraged Financing.

Raghu-nomics Specialty: Markets as a Whole

These considerations become possible once we view the market as a whole. This is the specialty of Raghu-nomics. We provided this same kind of birds-eye view for healthcare and immigration. That is what makes our assessments so different over other 'experts.' It's our basic template for assessing market dynamics and the natural reforms born of this perspective.

Politicians insert themselves and try an repackage these as political issues, but they are economic in nature. This Raghu-nomics formula is far more effective at tackling such issues over today's political postures that now lead the country's conversation. As such, our programs outperform other reforms now proposed by Washington. The political firestorm over these issues of healthcare and immigration has offered us a spectacular platform to introduce our Raghu-nomics programs. Welcome to Raghu-nomics.

You-tube Video

https://www.youtube.com/watch?v=UOwIkiJRPa8&t=2s

Edit Notes & other scraps

***

Each of these partners also bring their own set of benefits. **Once combined, you beget an EXPONENTIAL impact upon debt reduction and value creation.**

For example:

a) Each new partner / product was build upon the one before it. In other words, there is a direct link between each so-called new product. It would be more accurate to say that the US mortgage process is more like an eco system rather than some random and 'different' financial products. We can only come to understand it once we see the whole of its eco-system. More on that shortly.

b) There was 10 different *Partners*. Each *Partner* paid on their respective policies / debts.

c) Much of that $65 trillion (80%) in *CDS* presents one of the most dramatic examples of *Mirror Debts*. It comes with a whole slew of new considerations. For example, there appears to be 5 CDS for every home mortgage. However, once combined, they would be the equivalent of a single policy against the entire real estate market.

d) Each new partner multiplies the market dynamics and often, presented the prospects for entirely new industries.

    i)   The *C-Dels* Insurance program is but one example. *(C-Dels: Chronicles of Debt Ledgers)*

    ii)   The Blockchain industry may prove even bigger then this C-Del market – among other new markets and industries to be spawned here.

****
___

That means there is just half the estimated debt. Every program would then be refinanced for just half its present debt. Each

. The would be refinanced ased upon the remaining amount

There would be an easy way to do this. Refinance all old mortgages from 2008. The price would be set by adding up all the *Double Write-downs*. Sub-track that amount from the total outstanding Phantom Debt left throughout all 3 Groups. We only count their real estate holdings and subtract from that. We than refinance all those old homes at the reduced costs of the total debt.

Example

That would reduce the total cost

today. he easy step to do this would be get a general view of

We will detail and breakdown each of these areas further later, but we can now have some general scope LEDER (Leverage Debt Reduction) can offer in reducing some of the trillions in America's debt load.

Here are 3 of several kinds of bail-outs the gov't provided to banks:

a) There was the direct $1 trillion bail-out during the first weeks of the 2008 market collapse.
b) The Federal Reserve and US Treasury continued buying more 'Securities' (on the side) in the months and years after that.
c) 'Quantitative Easing' was just another fancy name for buying even more real estate securities.

US Bonds were the final step of this mortgage process. All the other Partners came before the gov't converted them into bonds. Most every other Partner had taken large 'pay-downs' on their holdings. None of those 'Double Paydowns' were ever added to the gov't debts.

By the time the gov't The gov't had bonds that had already been written far more than the That means that any pay-downs by previous Partners would reduce the debt amount for these US Bonds. In other words, *Double Paydown* is best reflected in US Bonds.

We hear all about the $20 trillion in Fed deficits. About 25% of that - $5 trillion - is *Phantom Debt*. Linking these US Bonds back to their original mortgage would allow us to tap the *Double Paydown*. Trillions of our federal deficit would evaporate - overnight.

Let's not forget the point of all this.

Different *Groups* & Different *Partners*.

Same mortgage debt.

It's just like your student loan. It was listed under your account as well as your mom and dads. It's still that same student loan. It's not an additional capital debt for each of you. Similarly, each of these *Partners* were only carrying mirror copies of the same original debt – your mortgage. Yes, counted under different names. Same mortgage.

Let's cover the first two *Groups of Partners* next.

The system follows the journey from your home mortgage over to Wall Street. It than tracks all the *'Double Paydown'* and applies them to your home mortgage, to Wall Street investments and to the US Bonds in their final phase as Fed Deficits.

* ... * ... *

Of course, there's the (in)famous student loan. Their Double Paydowns are already tracked and credited. However, the total volume of *Phantom Debt* in student loans should be quantified. How much of that debt is made of co-signers? Clarifying this will likely resize this behemoth into less then we presently think.

* ... * ... *

Market Pairing – 2008: there were as many homeless as there were available homes from foreclosure. Filling the homes with homeless – covered by gov't, would have stabilized markets for far less then the trillions in bank bailouts.

Chapter 2: Duplication - How It Works

Most have a sense how this would be true of financial markets, but would be surprise is to learn how this is also true for everyday business as well. A more obvious example would be a developer. He takes a loan to buy a $50,000 lot and hire a contractor to build a $100,000 home. That contractor goes to take out a loan of his own to buy materials and hire subcontractors – plumber, electrician, etc. Each sub-contractor then goes off to also take out loans for materials and additional manpower. The construction workers know that they have work so they also go and burrow money from their credit cards. Home Depot and the other suppliers and stores have this new wave of buyers so they too go and take out additional credit lines to fill the new inventory demand. That developer with

$150k housing project may generate $500k worth of 'Mirror Loans' between all the contractors, construction workers and stores.

The only value backing up this $500k worth of new debt is that $50k piece of land the developer is buying. We now have 10 x more debt then that land is worth. On the face of it, it appears that we could never – ever –pay-off that $500k worth of debt with this one $50k piece of land. That is what we are hearing today from all these financial experts that are setting off alarm bells how we have 10 x the debt then our nations GNP. That would be like looking at the credit reports of each contractor, supplier and worker as a separate and unrelated debt. This They are missing the common

This is what we have today when we hear the professionals telling us

Each player is actually borrowing against that one plot of land.

If we looked at all of these all of this debt was looked at separately

takes a loan out to hire materials and other contractors. The homeowner has taken out a loan to hire the contractor who then also takes out a loan to buy materials

Here's were 'Leverage Debt Reduction' comes into play. Let's say you pay-off $20,000 worth of your student loan. That $20,000 payment actually write-off's $60,000 worth of debt. $20,000 of debt is paid-off from your mom's credit report, another $20k from your dads and again the same for your own. Remember the $150,000 in combined debt when each of your credit reports were counted separately? Well, that combined debt falls to just $90k with your single $20,000 payment. You made one payment, but it pays down the debts listed under 3 different names– you, your mom, and your dad. Each account will see this debt reduction on their credit report.

Leverage Debt Reduction suggest that this kind of duplication can be found throughout a host of areas of today's financial system. This is true of the seemingly impossibly large sums of debt and of both the vast sums of listed debt and the ability of paying of

It's much easier to track debt obligations for co-signers of student, house or biz loans. We suggest it's time we have a similar tracking system in place for Credit Default Swaps and other derivative products. Doing so would allow us this same kind of debt resolution.

- * *
- One value, from our student loan example, is having 3 different people guarantying and paying on that loan. Put another way, there is the income from 3 different people serving as a back-up to that same loan. We had this in 2008. There was 7 different parties paying on the same debt. Each of these 7 parties had their own assets to back up their debt obligations. Tracking their combined input would have uncovered a far greater paydown on the loans.
- Another value from our student loan example, would be you graduating. Say you are now an attorney. You have the capacity to make $90k a year. Again, this too was at play in 2008. There was a genuine value added built in to the housing market. The bulk of the defaults on the mortgages, for example, was due to the sudden spike in interest rates. Low credit buyers were given 'subprime mortgage. They came with a low introductory interest rate. By year 3 or 4, the interest rate would double or triple from a low like 3% to a very high 11%. These interest jumps were behind 70% of ALL defaulted loans. The experts blamed 'subprime' buyers with low credit scores rather than on these rate spikes used on low income buyers. In other words, 70% of the entire real estate bubble could have been sidestepped by simply pausing those interest rate spikes. Greedy bankers would not hear of it and so we had the entire system implode. Has there ever been a greater example to the cost of greed. $20 trillion in global values lost within months. This is one of dozens of such examples where small steps would have easily maintained a healthy real estate market.
- We can find such simple measure once we have b
- We just need to track the value each of you have by way of income and assets and any and all paydowns made by any one of you. This is what was

missing from the 2008 market meltdown. We failed to see the value in assets and income and multiple paydowns that were there We referred to the ease of the issue of 2008 as 'an accounting mistake.' (Video below).